Relativity

·

Relativity

Dwight L. James

Writers Club Press
San Jose New York Lincoln Shanghai

Relativity

Writers Club Press
an imprint of iUniverse, Inc.

For information address:
iUniverse, Inc.
5220 S. 16th St., Suite 200
Lincoln, NE 68512
www.iuniverse.com

Any resemblance to actual people and events is purely coincidental. This is a work of fiction.

ISBN: 0-595-22191-2

Printed in the United States of America

for lewis and teresa

Contents

Contents

Prologue

tranquility

there is power in silence—it gives us the ability to observe, to listen and to think. we have all, at some point in our lives, been guilty of assuming that those who are silent are passive and weak. i have an admiration towards those who find peace in silence, because they are comfortable and at peace with themselves—mind, body and spirit. they don't have to present themselves to feel presentable nor do they have to prove themselves to feel proven.

maybe we should all aspire to be silent at some point in our lives. it can be for a second or a minute, but having a piece of mind may rest within our tranquility. ultimately, a piece of mind will grant us the composure and calmness to deal with adversity, while others may find the truth to questions that our mind cannot answer alone.

struggle

we all have differing personalities vying for some measure of achievement within our lives. some come at just the right moment, while in other situations, our aspirations and our fondest hopes find little support in our environment. very few people can truly say they are living their lives exactly according to their desires. for the majority of us, life is a series of conflicts between our inner ideas and outer constrictions.
goals are important, but so is forbearance. without it, we cannot know any

true meaning in our accomplishments. of course, when things happen without struggle, it does not mean that we didn't deserve it.

a musician may compose a brilliant peace in an afternoon, a writer may write a beautiful poem during one sitting, and people may say, "it happened so fast!" but in reality, it took many years of dedication and struggle to come to that moment of climax. even the grandest performance is the tip of a lifetime of struggle, and the basis of one's achievement is a mental journey of long perseverance.

success

i am often reminded that success is not tangible. it is a journey and not a destination. success is not precluded by an honorary distinction, nor is it something that is measured by raises or promotions. success is just as much, if not more, internal as it is external. it lies within the individual—it nests within their heart and mind propelling them to achieve in life.

Acknowledgements

the willing servant

guide me so that i may journey
develop me so that i may lead
invoke me so that i may inspire
fulfill me so that i may pray

call me so that i may serve
humble me so that i may appreciate
balance me so that i may aspire
free me so that i may express

i'm asking you to provide me with light
i pray that you will influence me to do the things that are
    right
Lord, there are times when doing right seems like the
    wrong thing to do
if i am worthy, i beg you to mold me into the image of
    you

your servant in Christ—

amen

knowing pain

when i saw the leaves drift away i hurt inside
they seemed lost and tormented, somewhat fragile and
   frail as the wind carried them to their new destination

why did they leave
were their roots of foundation removed or did their seed
   of fertility omit itself from the springtime of life that
   the leaves may have been looking for

regardless, it pains me
my heart aches when something or someone is left behind
   with their arms or branches outstretched only to be
   repressed by neglect

although love may be present, it may lack the mutual
   bond of sensibility that evokes the feeling of closeness
   between two

reflecting on the differences between love and pain
   prompted me to notice the leaves once more, while
   trying to determine their future destination

transitional diversion

emotionally i am without remorse or regret
tantalized by caution and change while losing focus and
    motivation

i feel lost and alone…

…where does this leave me?

holding on to promise and subjection
knowing that my transition into acceptance has reached a
    premature pinnacle

what i need cannot be defined or constructed
what i yearn for is neither historic nor fictitious

i want the happiness that lacks the infinite measurement
    of time
the happiness that removes sorrow and relinquishes joy

my life is not futile
spiritually i am removed
praying to be replenished by the life i once had

relativity

i can't explain it but i don't want to
the passion for this relativity has left me confused

why do i miss you and i barely even know you—what
    does this mean
touching you and holding you seem premature but
    comforting you inspires me
your eyes have told me your story
say nothing more

it has been left without disregard knowing that only you
    and i can prevent what our friends have labeled as
    destiny

the way we met
the way we looked at each other
the way we vibed with each other

it can only be defined as different to you and unique to
    me
but i like it—
my dear, i want to eventually love it

you knew i would be gentle because my eyes, like yours,
    told a story
i won't harm you

did my fingers lie as i caressed you
did my embrace mislead you when i held you
did my presence offend you when i got close to you

.

you would be surprised where this type of passion could
    lead
longing for each other in nights of loneliness and solitude
    in the humidity of our own sweat
stimulated by the caloric sensation of the sweet nectar
    within your inner thighs
and the pulsating rush of charismatic enigma that
    embellishes me

i don't consider myself to be the average brother—
fuck those other men
i want to be more than your lover
i'm about actions and words
to hell with dollars and rings
that will eventually come
but right now…

…i want you to understand *me*

have i gone on a tangent expressing how i feel for you
i could lie about my emotions but i don't want to
especially since i've promised that i would never lie to you

if time stood still

what would you do

images of love

hidden emotions pour from my eyes

beneath my soul is a sacred place forbidden to all that is
    impure

it leaks compassion and misery
wounded by love and tainted by misguided trust

my soul was once my imagination
a platform for commitment destined to parallel our
    universe

the collaboration of our love was once synonymous with
    creation
an act of God that would forever change the world

now i am left with our memories
a consolation of images that once were but will never be
    again

although our lives have grown apart
my love for you will forever remain the same

passionate influence

her lips persuade me
without voice
without sound

coerced by the thought of a previous encounter
manipulated by the anxiety of anticipation
the rites of passion preclude our discussion
discounting the importance of conversation and
    introduction

preempting the longing for bodily pleasure and climatic
    sensations
i have no choice but to surrender who i am
to become what she wants

i am

feeble
in her presence

misguided
when i feel her touch

disillusioned
when i hear her words

spare what hope is left within me
preserve a passion that is pure
not soiled with disdain and mistrust

allow me to rekindle my own beliefs
without the distortions created by her envy and self-
    righteousness

i am torn
        between
my journey for love
        and
her contentment with infatuation

season of romance

birds chirping
children playing
sun smiling
clouds crying
flowers blooming

springtime

until there was you

what you've shown me is immeasurable

i didn't know
if i could love someone the way they loved me

i didn't understand
the meaning of the word cherish

i didn't appreciate
the value of the word devotion

i didn't recognize
the comfort of the word commitment

i didn't have
the desire to experience the appreciation that others share
daily

i didn't want
to be a part of anyone's happiness except my own…

…*until* i met you

God has touched us with his blessings and i am constantly
reminded of our happiness when i look into your eyes

please understand my position—

i am in love with you

what i feel for you will remain greater than anything
    eternal because you are the consummate joy of my life

...because of time?

where are we left to go when *time* betrays us—
at what point will it befriend our paths
can we reconcile our differences or wait until another *time*
i want our relationship to last

how should we react when *time* belittles us—
is maturity the only answer for a lack of judgment
is it possible to overcome our realities of insufficiency
should we continue and possibly lose the faith that we
     covet

what do we say when *time* humbles us—
will possibilities and dreams become limited
would we recognize our flaws of expression
while failing at becoming more committed

can we blame *time* for our imperfections—
should wrongdoings prevent someone from believing
if the true essence of what we are trying to accomplish in
     time is eternal happiness
then what exactly are we achieving

what do YOU offer?

it bothers me when i hear women complain about finding
a man that can fulfill their needs
a man that makes a good living, is emotional, honest and
oh yes who can plant his seeds
a man that will rub his woman's shoulders and give her
bubble baths at night
a man that will seduce his woman's body and mind when
his fingertips are ripe
a man that will listen to his woman, making her feel safe
and secure
a man that will express his emotions, helping his woman
realize that he is willing to endure
a man that will pray for his relationship during setbacks
and misgivings
a man that will feel ashamed of his wrongdoings even
though he has been forgiven

if all of these qualities for a man are truly what a woman
is seeking
what would she do if she found this man—would she love
him or mistreat him
there are several men who offer these qualities in a
relationship with a woman
yet she rarely reciprocates these qualities to him at any
given moment
"he's too nice" or "he's too good" is what she tells her
girlfriends from time to time
but FYI: 'you don't have to be a roughneck to spank your
woman from behind'

what about the times when your workday seems
    unbearable and frustrating
only to come home and find that he has dinner already
    waiting
before a woman criticizes about what men are not willing
    to do
understand that the qualities that you're looking for in us
    we're also looking for in you
if you have a man that offers you complete happiness
    until there is nothing left
you better love that man with those same qualities or
    you'll soon wake up by yourself…

the extension of my love

the extension of my arms represents several things -
my feelings toward you
my inner thoughts about you
my fondness of finally seeing you

our embrace defines the honesty of our emotions and the
purity of our relationship
the trustworthiness of our time together and our
faithfulness while apart

this is my extension—a definition shaped by standards
that reach beyond a lifetime

it encompasses time and our journey together
whether in conjunction or miles apart

if my embrace seems longer than expected—forgive me…

…for i have missed you and my extension reaches far
beyond the physical temperament of this moment

soaking in this reality has created an imagery of time not
spent

my embrace speaks of love in infinite languages that can
be translated instantaneously

the manifestation of this love has taken an eternity to
create

a woman battered

as i look in my mirror, i notice the wrinkles in my face,
    scars on my chest and bruises beneath my robe

my body is weak because my past has altered my mind
    and taken the life out of my soul

glimpses of realism flash before me reminding me of
    better days filled with love and moments of giving

that same past is what has destroyed my dreams and as a
    result i have no reason for living

i prayed to God during my turmoil, but i suffered, so i
    wondered was God really listening

reciprocity, generosity, and love were what i once believed
    in but it was obviously missing

did "I" not give enough—was it something in the way "I"
    acted or something in what "I" was saying

was he not ready for my love and the feelings that my
    heart was desperately conveying

if only i would have adhered and followed the advice of
    those who told me to listen

i would not be behind these walls viewed as a murderer,
    but instead, embraced as a victim

the window

outside my window lies a memory
it has the appearance of many faces
pain
happiness
heartache
love

keep your words to yourself

watching you like a tiger piercing at its prey
i predict your movements by the motion
each day i time our encounter by the second
(in case you're wondering it's seventy-two)

i don't know your name
but i don't want to
i don't have your number
but i don't care

a glance from you is all i need
look into my eyes and see beyond what your rational
    mind will tell you
if it's not mutual
i will understand

when you look at me your actions will give me your
    answer
if you can't express yourself please keep quiet
i don't want your words…

if my fate came before me...

...would i question my actions and decisions when i look
    back in time
what would be the questions that circulate in my mind

did i make peace with my enemies and offer advice to my
    friends
did i give someone help even though i would never see
    them again
did i change someone's life when they were troubled and
    led astray
did i offer someone a future that had been denied a way
did i offer love and compassion at the crossroads of
    hostility
were my contributions worthwhile to both my family and
    my community

did i respect people as i would have wanted them to
    respect me
did i fulfill promises to those that i loved even though
    they never loved me
did i achieve the goals bestowed upon me by my history
    and my past
did i truly honor my ancestors when i wanted to fight
    instead of laugh
did i share my tears with others when my emotions were
    needed
was i humble in my accomplishments or did i seem brash
    and conceited

did i mistake my job and my money for happiness and
prosperity
did i consider the life of the poor man who found God
and reality
if all of my decisions regarding my past were ever brought
into question
when God confronts me during my judgment will he still
grant me all of his blessings

never-ending

like wine pouring from a bottle
my emotions flow freely
despite past failures at love
the pursuit shall remain endless

untitled

longing for her presence has defined me
my thoughts
my decisions
my actions
my consequences

sensual illusions will remain a physical mystery

unless

i

see her
feel her
taste her
live her

seeing you again

can i see you again…

…i never had the chance to step to you
was it my lack of courage that wouldn't allow me to
should i have noticed you sooner, but what would that do
me waiting for the right moment made me desire you

can i see you again…

…thinking of you makes me envision a sexual fantasy
should i apologize for my appreciation of your sensuality
if so, then i'm sorry—will you forgive me
if not, then you've answered my question about your
    personality

can i see you again…

…i don't want my eagerness to become an obsession
if i stated my intentions would you feel that i'm too
    aggressive
if so, this once, would you make me an exception
your body is my prize although i don't view you as a
    possession

can i see you again…

...all of this waiting is filling me with frustration
you not understanding how i feel has put me in an
    awkward situation
this ordeal has made me come to the realization
that seeing you again has become a figment of my
    imagination

shattered dreams

left without sorrow
neglected
hurt

afraid to…
trust
hope
love
believe
dream

again

steps

one by one i become synonymous with progression
a non-traditional pilgrimage defined by perseverance and
    not religion
immersed with the offerings of life and the attainment of
    worldly possessions
seen through the windows of the soul

each step becomes idealistic and each goal becomes more
    materialistic
the ladder seems sturdy
my mind has become frail

an imbalance in perfection overwhelms me
yet i become comfortable with the height in which i have
    climbed

the crossroads of rationality alter my purpose
stimulating my consciousness of obligation

what i'm seeking is mental

when emotions are present and not expected
when we can have discussions without speaking
when 'it' is a verb and not a noun
when honesty is understood and not requested
this is the type of love i am seeking

when expressions are portrayed and not left unsaid
when we can cry without hurting
when we can make promises without apprehension
when we can make love without having sex
this is the type of love i am seeking

when trust is given and not taken away
when we can find solace without being in each other's
    presence
when commitment is viewed as progression and not as a
    threshold
when desire becomes less carnal and more emotional
this is the type of love i am seeking

appreciation

i only knew what i felt
words were not important to me at the time

the thought of her caressing the side of my face while i
    endured pain
was far more heartwarming than any phrase or expression
    that i could ever imagine

she knew how i felt even though my words were lost
my only means of communication with her was a voice of
    agony and suffering
        unthinkable by the average man
        unbearable to the average person

a moment of comfort was what i needed…

…as she held me, i heard a light voice whispering in my
    ear
suddenly there was silence
i rose from her shoulder and looked at her eyes as if this
    were a defining moment in my life

for some reason my pain began to ease as my thoughts
    began to grow
it was evident that i was not alone
emotionally, i knew it was her that alleviated my hurt and
    tamed my fears

once i began to speak my voice crumbled
weakened from the pain that preceded me
damaged from the agony that nearly destroyed me

she grinned indicating her encouragement showing a sign
of faith
as the words began to flow from my lips
my confidence had been restored
my emotions had been repaired

she was the source for my restoration
since that day i have never been the same
for this reason i hold her close to me even when she is not
there
this is why i love her
this is why she is my friend

forever is only the beginning

give me your dreams—i want to parallel them with your
heart as long as time will permit

i want to emerge as your fantasy and become the man you
believed would never exist

may i grant you my soul in a spiritual union

spending a lifetime together is not enough for me

i want you to experience the daily consumption of my
love

beyond the days we rest in peace

how imaginative i've become since our initial encounter
many sun rises and moon falls past

i don't want to be the first man that adores your presence
and admires your beauty

i want to be the last

i know my words seem forward

to you that may be an unwarranted form of aggression

if that is what it takes for me to have hope of a future
between us

you will soon see that my love transcends affection

speaking of affection, do you have any idea of the sexual
tension that my body has been feeling

during sleepless nights i visualize my tongue tracing your
inner and outer thighs

as your facial expression becomes unyielding

oh yes—i fantasize about us often

the places we could go and the things that we could do

my lips against your lips and my fingers caressing your
breasts

the only words i want to hear are that you want me inside
of you

a soul without hope

i stand before darkness in a world that lacks meaning
internal strength cannot propel me
knowledge and determination no longer compel me
extending my arms to heaven while living in hell
tormented in a reality of misgiving

when you know who you love

immersed, nothing is ever rehearsed—spontaneity invites
  me
it enlightens me and gives me hope of what we might be
taken by storm caught in a raft
living each moment to experience the next laugh
speechless by chance never by choice
thanking God for your beauty, your smile and your voice
never question emotion, i want to offer you devotion
i'm not like most guys trying to ride the waves in your
  ocean
can you feel my rhythm, are you with my vibe, don't diss
  me now 'cause i'm on a natural high
herb can't do this for me, can't you see
you're my root and my love for you is our tree
moments of passion leave me impaired mentally
this emotional attachment has consumed me and
  removed me from reality placing me in a higher galaxy
where people don't reside, they only remain
i'm waking up in the middle of the night screaming out
  your name
am i insane?
NO! i am in love
no regrets no issues
when we're together i still miss you
i always want to kiss you
because of my emotional attachment
my God i can't believe this is happening
i once thought loving someone like this would be a life
  filled with madness

not gladness or reverence, a soothing feeling of
   benevolence
i don't want to live if my life will be any less than this

your smile

i see your smile

when the wind blows and the birds fly
when nature unfolds
when clouds cry
when i listen to jazz and it eases my mind
when i open champagne
when i taste wine

i see your smile

when i tasted your lips and it healed my pain
when we made love
when you whispered my name
when i think about us spending time together
when you called me 'always' and when i called you
    'forever'

i see your smile

when i can't sleep at night
when i feel alone
when you gave me encouragement
when you made me strong

i see your smile

when i go to church and hear the choir sing
when i told you, "i believe in prayer."
when you said, "i believe in the same thing."

i see your smile

when i look in the mirror and i can see
when i first smiled at you and when you first smiled at me

∂ream or reality

visions of you staring at me
pacing and contemplating

i want you to come closer
my body needs you
don't hesitate any longer
i know what you're trying to do to me

the way you look at me stimulates my craving for your
    moisture against my frame
i want to trace the shadow of your silhouette

why do i keep envisioning you tasting me as you undress
    me
i can't help but visualize your body's orgasmic rhythm
    while your legs are wrapped tightly around my waist

yet, you're only staring at me

5

the endlessness of your skin
the enticement of your fragrance
the image of your silhouette
the invitation of your voice
the nector beneath your waist
i've lost my senses

sent by the gods of nature

your soul has become my resting-place
i have longed for you and prayed for you to the gods of
    nature

i asked apollo for you to shine in my darkness
guiding me and inspiring me to believe

i asked poseidon for you to comfort me when i cry
that my tears may flow like a river

i asked aeolus for you to carry me
exposing me to a new destination in the wake of time

i asked hephaestus for you to stimulate me
igniting my burning fire for your physical satisfaction

i asked eros for you to love me
as i will forever love you

perception

why have you made this an issue
you're complaining about the way i look at you

i can't help that i enjoy the pleasures of a woman's chest
keep in mind, i'm not the one showing the world both of
    my breasts

should i think any less…maybe not, but i will think
    differently
when you're wearing mini-skirts on a body that's a size six
    and your outfit is a size three

what are you really trying to prove or better yet what are
    you trying gain
yet you get upset at 'my boys' for not calling you by your
    name

girl please, i'm tired of you complaining about how
    disrespectful men are acting
when maybe that is attributed to the type of men that
    you've been attracting

is it worth it—is it something you want to endure
when the root for this whole madness lies within you
    feeling insecure

you're constantly saying, "i want you to appreciate my
     body as well as my mind"
well i will sweetheart if you put some clothes on from
     time to time

yet for some reason you're still concerned with how i
     perceive you
even though you're wearing a top that's see through

understand, by no means do i condone physical action
simply by the way a woman dresses or even how she is
     acting

right or wrong i do admit that i will form a perception
of what a woman wants and what she may be expecting

the next time a guy calls you by something other than
     your name
before you get upset and before you feel unrestrained

take a look in the mirror to see what you're portraying
in most cases it correlates with his impression of you and
     what he is saying

a common evolution

engulfed by expectations without the benefit of promise
consumed with ideas that persuade the nature of sincerity
     that once presided within you
convinced that societal elements have identified your path
no longer viewed by the eyes of those who know
left with a precept of success without understanding what
     you have truly become

i know not

i know not where the wind blows
or how it carries when it's cold
when the sun is distant and the sky is grey
the time when springtime seems so far away

i know not where people's emotions lie
or why we're most emotional when others cry
when the rain pours and sorrow pervades
at the time when trust is so often betrayed

i know not why others fail to smile
or why happiness, to some, seems less worthwhile
when the sun radiates during the summer season
the moment when life offers more emotion than reason

i know not where love prevails
or how it wins when it seems to fail
when clouds surround everything we have harvested
i suppose is the moment when love has truly started

a way of living

if i tell you
life is infinite
would you believe me
if not
what would you see
does it matter what you have been taught
since you were three
is it more of what you perceive

when i suggest
you should live more freely
would you take my advice
or disregard my theory
why is it so hard for you to believe me
is it hidden somewhere in your mind's reality

false pretenses

the first encounter
the eye contact
the flirtatious smile
the vibrance and the interest
the 'newness' of living

all of which serve as a pre-cursor to another journey
without traveling

another step
without climbing

"patience" no longer resides in our judgment nor does the
    concept of 'taking it slow'

the words are too often said but rarely practiced…

…so we move forward, basing a lifetime on a fraction

the thought of being mislead never preempts our
    expectations

the notion of possible heartache rarely succumbs to our
    thirst for companionship

we drink from the fountain of promises—"i love you's"
  and "i miss you's"…

…we hold onto the initial encounter and the way it made
  us feel
the way the phone sounded when we first heard it ring

did we really know who was calling or why

i know what they SAID but what did they *truly* MEAN

now we dwell on what was and what could have been, and
  wonder "why me"

i want a woman

who understands me
my needs and my insecurities
who doesn't question me
making me relive past relationships and heartaches
who will console me
helping me realize that my pain is her pain
who respects me
honoring our relationship and its commitment
who trusts me
seeing distance apart as growth not as deceit
who can relate to me
connecting with my innermost thoughts and most
    intimate details
who is willing to accept me
for who i am and not the person that she can change me
    into

i simply want a woman who will love me for me

the art of seduction (Part I)

i felt like i knew her even though we never met
sometimes i sit alone trying to visualize being with her in
sensual ways
unimaginable to the common person

our paths have only crossed twice in her lifetime
however, we have enjoyed far more moments in mine
i vividly remember one of those moments as if it were
yesterday…

…she was alone, standing on a balcony in the pouring
rain embracing mother nature

as the rain fell from the sky against her fragile frame
i envisioned caressing her body with an aggressive yet
delicate touch
while listening to her moan the cry of pleasure and
sensing her desire the art of seduction

my intuition convinced me to seize this moment of
climatic implication
by maneuvering my fingers amongst her body while
carefully positioning my lips against her breast

as the moment intensified, the thunder roared,
   resembling that of a lion in south africa
this moment of passion encompassed everything that a
   fantasy was meant to bring and embraced all the
   creativity that sexuality had ever become

i continued to caress my lips against her breast
tracing my fingers up her inner thigh towards her most
   sensitive area
enduring the rain as i felt it trickle down the side of my
   face
i began biting on her neck and sliding down the middle
   of her body with my tongue

she then placed her left leg over my right shoulder and her
   right leg over my left shoulder
as if she had intentions preceding any thoughts i may have
   imagined

at that point she grasped the balcony rails and reared her
   head back with her eyes closed as if she were holding
   on for her life

once i began tasting her sensitivity, she released a cry of
   passion indicating to me the feeling of ecstasy that my
   tongue was able to bring her

the rain continued to pour, sliding down her body
   through the crease of her inner thighs rolling down the
   side of my lips

she began shouting the words "make love to me" as the
  thunder echoed in the distance
as i arose, she took both of her hands and ripped open my
  shirt
desiring this moment of unity that we were both about to
  experience

sliding her hands down my body, she placed her fingers
  around my pleasure ever so gently
arousing my desires and stimulating my emotions

once she placed me inside of her, i began to feel the
  moisture of her sensitivity
embracing the essence of my pleasure while her legs were
  wrapped tightly around my waist
our movements were diligent yet passionate
thus exemplified by her nails clawing into my back

running my fingers through her hair
biting her neck as she said my name
penetrating in and out of her body as she moaned were
  only temporary
this moment, however, would last forever...

a token of love

nestled beneath my shoulder lies a treasure
it has been referred to as an organ by science
a token by humanitarians
a symbol by medieval historians

seldom looked upon for guidance
it can compel us to garner our emotions
such containment yields emotional complexity
influencing our actions despite what we may already
  know
it is beyond understanding and comprehension to this
  world and all that resides within it

lost innocence

there comes a point in life when moments are defined by
expression

my life has taught me that time is only a component of
my progression

throughout my life i wonder and search for answers
conveying the truth

it is not WHAT i become but WHO i become for me to
lose

i have betrayed my innocence and my principles for
success and monetary gain

the irony of my life's story is that improvement does not
always constitute change

i miss knowing that life is simple and that success is not
defined by stature

that notion is forever lost in time, and it is my innocence
that i will never recapture

you once asked me to define love

it doesn't take a poet to give a reason
why love is the only emotion that commemorates seasons

it is difficult to embrace in every situation
from previous infidelities and advantageous
   manipulations

we fail to realize the true essence of love's intentions
when it alters our desires and changes our inhibitions

if there is a definition for love, it exists within
through the birth of children and the fondness of friends

i know why

i know why you cry
when tears flow and pain resides
when love seemed distant
when there was nothing left to provide
i know why you cry

i know why you pray
when the relationship was troubled and you decided to
    stay
when your love wasn't enough for him and he went astray
i know why you pray

i know why

untitled

her presence magnifies beauty and justifies creation
smiling at her calms me
her mind stimulates my hunger for lifelong
    companionship

never circumvented by time
fearful of lacking time with her
one lifetime with her seems unfair
her voice echoes melodies of music that comfort my
    insecurities

she is my clairvoyant messenger of time

my reason
for living

my excuse
for never dying

a moment in our lives

a foundation between us has been laid without intent or
   purpose
it was only a few days ago that i didn't know you
days later i have become a part of your life and you of
   mine
wanting to see you is something that i cannot suppress

i missed you before i even left you
it is from this realization that i smile when i think of
   you...

...how we held and caressed each other before my
   departure
for those brief moments i became immersed in you
this immersion coerces me to visualize touching you and
   comforting your warmest needs

i am grateful knowing that i have shared a portion of my
   life with you
thank you for doing the same with me

my heart's vessel

my heart has been shipwrecked
piece by piece drifting upon secluded shores
my vessel has endured the tides and turbulent winds of
nature's forces

loving you now

distance never intruded what i perceived was real between
    us
time allowed me to persevere through the agony of
    depression without you

never unyielding
my belief in you
in us
the possibilities

i am now close to you in body
spirit
reality

the distance that once pervaded my mind no longer
    overwhelms me
i have been given the opportunity to love you

the risk of attraction

the basis of what i see in you defies everything that i have
    been taught
everything that i have read
everything that i believe

my attraction for you is not real
it can't be—i have lost my foundation of thought
my constant of reason
my trust in judgment

there are moments when i feel as though i have lost you
i miss the thought of us not sharing a moment together
a memory
a fraction in time

i have placed my heart in your hands
TAKE IT as you will
HOLD IT as if you need it to evolve

the presence of your spirit
consumes me when we are apart
the attraction for you will remain

i am left with my own sensibilities for loving
with the possibility of never being loved

a lesson in life

fallacies and lost realities once non-existent to me
purity not insecurity is the emotion that i once believed
positions of inhibitions have never constituted me as a
 man
trusting instead of lusting has made me into the person
 that i am

predictions and restrictions of my emotions were once
 misguided
the thought of something new and untainted no longer
 gets me excited
discouragement not encouragement is what altered my
 perceptions of expression
learning not everyone deserves my love has been my life's
 most valuable lesson

the thought of leaving

questions of honesty and commitment once clouded the
   ability to trust my lover

seclusion and isolation would not allow me to leave her
   for another

constant phone calls when night falls often negated the
   pleasantries of our evening

her ability to disillusion my disgust with reality forced me
   to question my motives for leaving

the constant agonizing when she was out past midnight
   receiving another lover's affection

often left me wallowing in my own insecurity when i
   should have been confronting her imperfections

attempting to soothe my pain existed in a cognitive
   fantasy of answers and solutions

becoming emotionally tired made me tormented by her
   inadequate contributions

regaining site of my purpose while restoring my identity

gave me courage to finally make leaving my relationship a
    reality

a physical appetite

my appetite has overturn me

the hunger that dwells inside of me manipulates the
   discomfort of my body and induces the anticipation
   that fuels my desire

as i reminisce about the fruits of pleasure imbedded
   within the touch of your fingertips, i realize that at
   some point my appetite must be fulfilled

longing for another chance to serve you properly has
   made me zealous
contemplating on how i can satisfy the regimen within
   me

lying here envisioning you makes me toss and turn

perspiration begins to flow from my body and moisture
   inevitably ripens beneath my waist

when can i taste the fruits of ecstasy again—

does your appetite lack fulfillment or is your sole purpose
   in life to fulfill me

regardless of your answer i want to facilitate our next
    encounter and relive that burning passion that i felt
    when your lips once consumed me

i won't hesitate at the table of thirst and hunger, because
    i will prepare for two only if that will be acceptable

just don't tease me with appetizers and finger foods
    because i want to eat more than 'snacks' and taste more
    than 'beginners'

be sure to remember the fruits and vegetables, and please
    my dear, don't forget the dessert

requests

i want to
wake up with you
touch you
caress you
smile at you
laugh with you
kiss you
undress you

i want to
grow old with you
console you
hold you
listen to you
cry with you
understand you
know you

i want to
love you

intentions

concurrent emotions massage the foundation of my
thoughts when i visualize your body's movements

my infatuation and desire for you influence
me—coercing my moral judgment and testing my
faith
creating a divine intervention

overwhelmed by sexual conviction creates an illusionary
world that will only be fulfilled by your presence

missing the "roundness" of your bosom inevitably makes
me yearn, craving the most illicit consequences of our
sexual togetherness

seeking clairvoyant guidance from your mystery has
confined me in this imaginary setting that we label as
myth

i am propelled beyond reality, stimulated by a thirst for
something physical

only to be left with erotic intentions

ɔelective imagery

collections of timeless images sit on my brain creating a
   memory of experiences in my former life

maintaining my imagery seems inevitable yet i try to
   overlook past miseries to reduce future heartaches

i must accept the truth of my reality and the fallacies of
   my imagination

hoping that my heart has mended so i may one day love
   again

as we grow together

like imprints in the sand, we have left traces of hope that
   true love does exist—

our paths have intertwined at the crossroads of
   opportunity—granting us the possibility to
   supplement a cerebral foundation that is pure and
   innocent

whispers of comfort breathe life into our
   souls—transcending our feelings and captivating our
   intuitions

a psychological beginning has levitated our hearts to a
   new horizon, overlooking the valleys and rivers that
   God once created

like nature, we have evolved from our purest elements to
   live freely—harmonious in the presence of peace and
   the contentment of tranquility

the culmination of our growth shall honor the trust that
   satisfies the balance of our existence

thus allowing us to love and cherish one another as each
   day passes by

forever, more than friends

i didn't anticipate creating passionate memories with you
that would sit indelibly on my mind

i often find myself frustrated between my naiveté of what
we are and my memories of how we once were

what do you see when you look at me—i have to know
because the memory of you has subsided within

does your body re-live my touch and how i am capable of
reducing the tension that has infiltrated your
shoulders and maneuvered beneath your waist

do you remind yourself of how the grace of my tongue
parts the passageway guarded by your breasts leading
me to your navel

do you often gasp during your reflection and recall the
moisture that develops in your most delicate areas...

...only to see me satisfy my thirst by carefully tasting
every inch of your skin

do you feel guilty imagining me, knowing your current
lover fails to fulfill your most desirable inhibitions and
your most inappropriate fantasies

i ask you, "friend", are your memories as collectible and
vivid as mine

all that i can offer

i offer you comfort...

...your pain is my pain

when you cry
i am your shoulder

when you fall
i am your brace

when you are tired
i will put you to sleep

i offer you support...

...together we can overcome adversity

when you walk
i will walk beside you

when you confront your fears
i will fight them with you

when you need help
my arms will extend to you

i offer you peace...

...your soul needs serenity

when you pray
i will pray with you

when you feel angry
my words will calm you

when you seem lost
your trust in me will guide you

i offer you love...

...i will give you all that i am and all that i hope to become

when you vow to be mine
i will be yours forever

we belong together because i know how it feels when
we're apart

this is what i offer you

temptation

i see you
out the corner of my eye
tempting me while *SHE* sits beside me

no repercussions?
no regrets?
maybe for you
not for me

yet you want to sit next to me
tell me how you would sex me
give me an oral preview of how you would taste me

i have journeyed down that path before—

now
i have reservations…

…of trips with no destination

reality

sometimes i laugh when i think about our past
i realize
now
why i loved you so much when we were together

i made mistakes -we both did
that was a part of growing up and maturing into the man
  and woman that we are today

i can't change what happened between us
God knows how much i would try

there was a point
when i tried to hate you
filling my heart with anger to rid myself of reality
regardless of how hard i tried
it never worked

people have experiences that change their lives forever
my dear
knowing and loving you has changed mine

untitled

clinging to every moment of our history
sunset fades upon my face
the realization of life alone beckons me to weep
my mind drifts along the hills of passion and rivers of
    tears

interwoven like a pattern
bound by love and promises
set free by hurt and disappointment

words

love
passion
desire
infatuation
obsession
adoration

words

pain
remorse
disappointment
frustration
drama
anguish

words

faith
hope
forgiveness
prayer
trust
opportunity

speechless

sexual resonance

please listen…
…to the harmonious sounds our bodies create

the moan of your voice
when i thrust my pelvis against your frame

the slap of my hand
against your backside

the bawl of your lungs
when i grab your hair

the gasp for breath
when i make you climax

the sigh of relief
when our composition is over

winning

finest cologne
new shirt
polished shoes
washed car

i'm gonna' win tonight

change the sheets
take down pictures
vacuum the floor
cut the ringer off

i'm gonna' win tonight

rent a movie
turn up the 'AC'
light candles
pull out a blanket

i'm gonna' win tonight

prepare the meal
pour wine
pour wine
pour wine
give a massage

i won last night

will you

will you ever respect me
look me in my eyes and tell me 'yo'
is my question irrelevant to you because i need to know
will you ever respect me

will you always lie to me
leading me to believe something that is untrue
while attempting to better myself, i often find myself
    helping you
will you always lie to me

will you always deny me
shaking my hand out of obligation
pretending that my credentials will improve your
    organization
inept to your intentions while enhancing my frustrations
will you always deny me

will you always fear me
demonstrated by your constant brutality
what was once shown by your overt nature has become
    your covert mentality
am i wrong because this is what my eyes see
will you always fear me

WILL YOU?

because of what you mean to me

i owe you my life because that is what you gave me

discipline and morality is what you imbedded, only to see
    me become a man in a society that is impure and
    corrupt

leaning on your trust and wisdom has made me
    appreciate both the recognition of success and the pain
    of misfortune

i pray i have become the son that you asked God for on
    the day of conception

emotional cure

my love
you massage the innermost anxieties that preside within
me

healing

my ailments of insecurity
my void for peace

art of seduction (part II)

still
i have not endured the luxury of meeting her
creating moments psychologically have become inevitable
images piece themselves like a pattern woven in my mind
each illusion is vivid
spawning the desire to live my fantasy

looking into the mirror of imagination
i reflect on our most recent encounter…

…it was a summer night with a slight breeze
she was lying in bed (asleep) with candles outlining her
    frame
her balcony door was left open as the moon watched her
    breath peacefully
satin sheets protected her hips and thighs while her
    shoulders and breasts remained bare and unguarded
her back glistened, shielding the rays of the moon from
    penetrating her body

admiring her beauty was sinful—
the lustful desires and primal cravings overwhelmed the
    angelic aura before me
i approached the bed with sexual intentions
each step towards her served as a stimulus for seduction

Relativity

my mouth began to moisten
prompting me to kneel down and kiss her
not wanting her eyes to open i proceeded to gently trace
    the border of her lips with my tongue
she let out a moan from the bellows of her abdomen
the cadence of her sound became dictated by my actions

i began exploring her body
with my eyes
with my hands
with my tongue

"please" she muttered—"i want you deep inside of
    me"—"make me scream"

lying between her thighs
i felt the warmth trying to escape her body
we became synchronized with our movements
rhythmic to the sounds of fulfillment
    moaning
        screaming
            sighing
                exhaling

About the Author

Born in South Carolina, Dwight L. James first began writing poetry at the age of twelve. He has published several poems and written one book, **On the Edge of Destiny**, which was published in June of 1997. He has received several awards for his poetry and has been recognized by many literary organizations, including The International Library of Poetry. Dwight sites several writers that have inspired his work including Paul

Laurence Dunbar, Carl Sandberg, James Baldwin and Pablo Neruda, to name a few.

Dwight received a B.A. from Morehouse College, and an MBA from Duke University, The Fuqua School of Business in. He currently resides in Atlanta, GA.

0-595-22191-2

Printed in the United States
894900004B